G.J.Ol...
70 Ha...
...ccington
BURY
Chriestmas 1997.

WRITERS' BRITAIN

ENGLISH CRICKET

In the same series

English Cities & Small Towns John Betjeman
English Villages Edmund Blunden
The English Poets Lord David Cecil
British Dramatists Graham Greene
Life Among the English Rose Macaulay
English Country Houses Vita Sackville-West
English Women Edith Sitwell

ENGLISH
CRICKET

NEVILLE CARDUS

with
8 plates in colour
and
14 illustrations in
black & white

PRION

This edition published in Great Britain by Prion
32-34 Gordon House Road
London NW5 1LP

Text copyright © 1945 the Estate of Neville Cardus
This compilation copyright © Prion 1997

First published in 1945 by Collins

All rights reserved.
No part of this book may be reproduced, stored in a retrieval
system, or transmitted in any form or by any means, electronic,
mechanical, photocopying, recording or otherwise, without the
prior written permission of the publisher and copyright owners.

A catalogue record of this book can be obtained
from the British Library

Colour origination by MRM Graphics, Singapore
Printed and bound in Singapore

NONE EXCEPT THE PEOPLE OF ENGLAND OR OF THE English-speaking countries has excelled at cricket. Other nations not obsessed by sport are able to hold their own with us at tennis, golf, football, but cricket is incomprehensible to them, a possession or mystery of a clan, a tribal rite. So it is, or something of the kind; for cricket is an institution and only a game incidentally – as the Poet Laureate might easily be a poet. Like the British Constitution, cricket was not made: it has 'grown.' Its rules and its general legal system tell of the English compromise between individual freedom and corporate responsibility; cricket is known as essentially a 'team-game,' yet one player may dominate the proceedings for hours, as much the cynosure of all eyes as a prima-donna. On the other hand, the greatest cricketer in the world will sooner or later find himself so anonymously just a part of the whole, the XI, that he is reduced to mute and inglorious inactivity for hours; his name even

Bradman, none the less the most obscure and inept of his colleagues may run him out for no runs even before he has been able to show his quality against a single ball. The team's destiny in a match might rest on somebody who all day has passed unobserved at deep long-on. So far he has had no opportunity to show that he is taking part in the match at all, except as a constituent in the colour scheme of greens and whites and yellows. Suddenly a huge hit soars aloft; the ball endomes the heavens. Deep long-on is now exposed and rendered notable. Where is the team-spirit now and its blessed brotherly influence and aid in this crisis? The ball hovers on high and maybe it descends spirally. And if the occasion is a Lancashire and Yorkshire match—and great hits to deep long-on have on occasion been known to occur in Lancashire and Yorkshire cricket matches—the crowd assembled immediately behind deep long-on is likely to call out, critical in cloth caps, 'He'll miss it; he'll miss it . . . there thou art; what did Ah tell thi?'

A collection of score cards faded with age, a volume of 'Wisden' yellow as autumn sunshine, will speak of the English climate and of the English summer's caprices. The hot days witness the processional movement of batsmen to their centuries; the wet days see them dispossessed, disenthroned, and of no account. The weather of England enters cricket like a *deus ex machina*. One warm Sabbath afternoon, brilliant with sunshine, following a thunderstorm at church-time, I was walking in Hyde Park when I met two famous Yorkshiremen—Wilfred Rhodes and Emmott Robinson. Yorkshire had batted at Lord's throughout Saturday and had scored nearly four hundred runs.

'It's cleared up nicely,' I said to the two old soldiers of Yorkshire as I greeted them. Emmott nearly snapped my head off.

'Aye!' he retorted, like a knife, 'and a sticky wicket goin' to wa-aste at Loards!' It was an attack on unnecessary Seventh Day observance.

There are better games, as games. Frequently there is no decision at all in cricket, sometimes scarcely a beginning. But it is on rainy days that the charm of the game has been known to work its most subtle spells for those who play country cricket, away from the bricks and mortar of Kennington and Leeds (both much beloved in their places). The vacant and rural field is shrouded in mist as you walk through the entrance-gate hoping against hope. There is a sound of footsteps on the wooden pavilion; perhaps there'll be play after all. Then the clouds are suddenly pulled apart, and the sun changes the grass to a field of jewels. And men in white appear from nowhere, and soon two little mounds of sawdust are placed at each end of the wicket and bowlers sometimes lose volition like boys on a slide, and the bat sends forth its ineffectual thud; while in adjacent trees the birds make busy noises, and aloft in the blue sky there are great castles on cliffs of clouds, and burning lakes. These things all belong to the game as much as the implements, the technical achievement, and the 'result.'

The foreigner is naturally baffled. He arrives in London and sees a newspaper poster: 'England's Danger.' An international crisis has occurred behind his back, during his journey from the Continent! No; but almost as important, six wickets have fallen at Lord's including that of Hammond, to the invading Australians.

Any savant examining *a priori* the evolution of cricket and its implements and law could easily fall into grave and far-reaching fallacies. The shape of the bat, to begin with—in the early days when cricket was mixed up with other of the nation's field-sports, and was patronised by the Fancy and went hand-in-hand with cock-fighting and gambling—in those bad old times, the cricket bat was crooked in shape, or at least it was curved. But in the high noon of Victorian respectability, after muscular Christians had incorporated the game into the curriculum of an English gentleman's education, why, by this time the bat was straight and of white willow made. Two sayings became liturgical almost, 'Play a Straight Bat,' and 'It's not Cricket.' (Meanwhile W. G.

Grace and A. N. Hornby were attending lustily to that rigorous battle of wits without which no national pastime is worth a moment's while.) In cricket's period of unashamed sowing of wild-oats, Tom Lockyer kept wicket for England, and one day in a match against 'Odds' he directed a batsman's attention to a displaced piece of turf on the pitch, right on the length. And when the young innocent walked out of his crease to remove the divot, Lockyer, ball in hand, whipped off the bails. His answer, when taken to task for sharp practice, was reasonable enough: 'You can't be too careful when playing twenty-two.'

IT IS FAR MORE THAN A GAME, THIS CRICKET. IT somehow holds the mirror up to English nature. We are not hypocrites, but we try to make the best of things of contrary appeal. It was once alleged that W. G. Grace now and again cheated. I asked an old Gloucestershire 'pro' to speak frankly on this subject. 'Nay !' he protested with proud emphasis, 'never. The "Old Man" cheat?– 'e were too clever for that.' We are expedient as a people, and not without humour. The history of cricket, made by Englishmen no more ethical than jockeys and pugilists and footballers, does justice like a play or a pageant to our national horse-sense, sentiment, and powers of accommodation.

The crooked bat became straight out of sheer

JOSEPH GUY 1857
'Elegance, all elegance, fit to
play before the Queen in her parlour.'

expediency: wit and not morality was the cause. A curved bat, with the weight concentrated at the bottom, was necessary as a counter to the ancient underhand bowling, quick and along the ground, almost 'grubs.' As soon as Hambledon men bowled a length and used the air and caused the ball to rise sharply from the ground, a hockey-stick sort of defence was of no avail, and so the shouldered narrow blade was evolved. Even this most hallowed of symbols of cricket, the straight bat, was not given its fair and narrowish rectitude by some categorical imperative issued from conscience and ethic; oh dear no ! In the beginning no bound was put by law on the width of a blade. One day a cricketer of Reigate came into action with a bat broader than the wicket. It is pleasant to imagine the scene in which this great opportunist of Reigate prepared his new weapon; the quiet kitchen in his cottage in the village; and while he smoothed and polished his handiwork with sandpaper until it glowed in the candle-light, he chuckled to his admiring wife: 'Hey old lady, but this be an artful device, and a march forward of the Intellect.' Alas for the vision that overreacheth, a rule was brought in enforcing a four-and-a-half inch limit. None the less, the Archimedes of Reigate—'Shock' White to his intimate friends—had his hour and it became immortal.

Three stumps pointing heavenward from the earth!—our savant would deduce from the first sight of them some show of Trinitarianism, especially in view of the large number of the clergy present at any cricket match on the field and off. But once again, the truth, the pragmatical truth, has to be confessed: the three wickets came into use and being only by the exigency that drives all of us, saints and sinners alike. In the Maytime of 1775 a fierce engagement took place between five men of Hambledon and five men of Kent. When the last man went in, fourteen runs were wanted for a Hambledon victory. 'Lumpy' Stevens, who was playing for Kent as a 'given man,' bowled through the wicket, defended by John Small—and the point is that the wicket then consisted of only two stumps with one bail like the crossbar of a gate. The frustration of 'Lumpy' as he beat John Small's bat time after time and saw the ball go vainly through the wicket, must have been awful and eloquently expressed, not only there and then but for long afterwards, in and out of season; for a third stump was added two years afterwards.

HAMBLEDON WAS NOT THE 'CRADLE' OF CRICKET. Kent played 'All England' on the 'Artillery' ground in London in June, 1744, and not for another ten years was the Hambledon Club much heard of, and it was 1786 before Hambledon met Kent and won. But the games on Broad-Halfpenny Down have been enshrined in the prose of John Nyren, who maybe received some literary aid from Charles Cowden Clarke. There is also Pycroft's *The Cricket Field*, the source of a tradition in literature which cricket shares with no other form of outdoor sport, unless Izaak Walton can be said single-handed to challenge it, supported by Jorrocks.

The Hambledon men bowled 'underhand,' and they wore dark breeches and snowy vests, silk stockings for the 'gentlemen.' It was not regarded as prejudicial to a cricketer of Hambledon's technical skill on the field if he could play the violin and sing in a sweet tenor voice away from it. Of 'Silver Billy' Beldham, of John Small who hung a sign outside his house:

> Here lives John Small
> Makes Bat and Ball,
> Pitch a Wicket, Play at Cricket
> With any man in England.

—of Tom Sueter, and Richard Nyren and David Harris, it would be superfluous to write here: and impossible even by dint of imagination and the most recently orchestrated prose style to improve on Nyren's panegyric of Beldham:

'It was a study for Phidias to see Beldham rise to strike, the grandeur of the attitude, the settled composure of the look, the piercing lightning of the eye, the rapid glance of the bat, were electrical. Men's hearts throbbed within them, their cheeks turned pale and red. Michael Angelo should have painted him. Beldham was great in every hit, but his peculiar glory was the cut. His wrists seemed turned on springs of the finest steel. He took the ball, as Burke did the House of Commons, between wind and water; not a moment too soon or too late.'

The dawn of the game was indeed as fresh as the herald of any summer day on the Hambledon Downs; it is as well to be in at the beginning of things before custom has staled, and before the law of diminishing returns has got to work. It is not sensible to ask doubtfully whether Beldham and Harris and their like would have been great cricketers in the company of Hammond, Bradman and Larwood.

I T IS BECAUSE CRICKET DOES NOT ALWAYS HURRY along, a constant hurly-burly, every player propelled here and there by the pace of continuous action, that there is time for character to reveal itself. We remember not the scores and the results in after years; it is the men who remain in our minds, in our imagination. Nobody asks what was the batting average of Joseph Guy, a Nottinghamshire cricketer of whom it was said by William Clarke, who got together and captained the first All England XI, that he was 'elegance, all elegance, fit to play before the Queen in her parlour.' Ponsford made more runs than R. H. Spooner—and there are more notes in a symphony by Shostakovitch than in one by Mozart. The man is the style at cricket.

We do not know, and we are not curious about the bowling averages of 'Lumpy' Stevens, who rose early on summer mornings at Hambledon to pick a wicket; for in those days the spin of a coin decided not only first innings but also gave the winner the right to choose the pitch. 'Lumpy' loved to send fast 'shooters,' and he invariably chose a wicket with a downward slope– 'for honest "Lumpy" did allow, He ne'er could pitch but o'er a brow.' Lineal descendents of 'Lumpy' were Emmott Robinson and Rhodes, who once inspected the wicket at Leeds after a wet morning. The sun was shining just before lunch, and Rhodes and Emmott pressed expert fingers into the texture of the turf. 'It'll be 'sticky' at four o'clock,' said Rhodes. Emmott pressed and fondled the turf again, then answered : 'No, Wilfred; half-past.'

The state of the turf is the clue to every cricket match; no other game comes as much under the influence of material circumstances; the elements are cricket's presiding geniuses. The wicket not only makes a valuation of skill, but also of character. A score of 100 for 3 might be good or ruinous, according to the state of the

Lords and Gentlemen of Surrey and Kent
playing at Knole Park, Kent, 1775

CRICKET MATCH BETWEEN NOTTINGHAM AND LEICESTER, c. 1829

wicket. A sudden fall of the barometer spells ruin—like a fall in securities on 'change. Bradman, when he is batting on a dry smooth lawn, and Bradman on a 'sticky' pitch, are only distantly related. One day he is the greatest run-maker ever known; to-morrow, possibly, he seems to go in to bat only that the scorers, like official receivers, may be supplied for accountancy's sake with the correct details of his bankruptcy. But Victor Trumper on his second visit from Australia to England, and during his first experience of a wet summer and spiteful English turf, and against the greatest spin-bowlers we have ever produced, made eleven separate hundreds, and, to quote the sober language of the *M.C.C. Cricket Scores and Biographies*, 'he hit on sticky wickets with freedom and scored well, often whilst his colleagues were puddling about the crease.' The season for him 'was one long triumphal progress, and those who were fortunate enough to witness his amazing brilliance will never be able to forget the unrivalled skill and resource he displayed.'

Not until we have considered the material conditions and environment of cricket—which include the implements, especially the heavy roller—can we measure exponent with exponent and period with period. Of the early Hambledon epoch we must be content to savour the character and the spirit; for technically the Hambledon game is scarcely linked even to the cricket of only fifty years afterwards. Hambledon men, as we know, bowled underarm; it was later than Hambledon, in May, 1828, when the M.C.C. legalised the round-arm action. The new rule permitted the hand to be raised as high as the elbow, and the arm to be extended outwards and horizontally. Seven years later, the law compromised again; the hand in delivering the ball could now be raised as high as the shoulder. As far back as 1788, Tom Walker of Hambledon had experimented with a round-arm action; but it was left to John Willes, in the year 1822, to wave the red rag of revolution under the nose of Lord's itself. He opened the attack for Kent against the M.C.C. and was promptly no-balled; and promptly he refused to play and got on his horse in dudgeon, and, as Mr. Altham says, rode out of Lord's and out of cricket history.

But the way was shown, and wide open now. The 'new' bowling became the rage at once; and a Sussex team, with Lillywhite in it, used round-arms so drastically that they thrashed All England twice in three matches. For thirty years to come, this bowling set the general technical stamp and provided the most important bridge passage in cricket's symphonic progress; it was cultivated to the highest possible potency by Alfred Mynn, Lillywhite, and Caffyn. Here was the beginning of 'modern' cricket.

But the Hambledonians apparently discharged

their bowling with characteristic vehemence. David Harris could cause an 'underarm' to rise abruptly from the pitch. He could 'grind a batsman's fingers against his bat.' Brett's attack was described as so 'tremendous' that Tom Sueter, the wicket-keeper, was acclaimed a hero because he could stump a man off Brett; and he wore no pads or gloves, nor did the batsman. The inexplicable point of style about the classic masters' underarm is their method of propelling the ball down the pitch, not with the lobbing action most of us moderns know, a variation of the quoit throw or the obeisance of the bowling green. Nyren describes how David Harris forced the ball away from the level of his armpit; and half a century later, Richard Daft tells of Clarke, 'at the last moment he bent back his elbow, bringing the ball almost under his right armpit...'

Brown of Brighton bowled underarm at such velocity that history asserts he killed a dog on the boundary; and the ball had passed through a coat held protectively by long-stop. But this event is dated round about 1818, after the sun set upon Hambledon. Probably Brown of Brighton was one of the stealthy advance guards of the revolution; I doubt if he killed his dog truly underarm, unless he bowled like Mr. Luffey who in *Pickwick* retired a few paces ('amid a breathless silence'), applied the ball to his right eye for several seconds, then cried 'Play!' whereat the ball flew straight and swift towards the centre stump of the wicket defended by Mr. Dumkins.

Yet, is it absolutely certain that on a Hambledon turf, against the underarms of David Harris and equipped and armed in the period's garb and implements, a tricorn hat on his head, the average contemporary batsman would find an innings of fifty runs child's play? In the Golden Age of batsmanship, on flawless wickets and in conditions as 'modern' as yesterday, Simpson-Hayward bowled lobs to the acute discomfort of stroke-players as sophisticated and brilliant and quick-footed as Johnny Tyldesley, A. C. Maclaren, David Denton; and in three Test matches in South Africa he took 21 wickets for 15 runs each, and he was coping with the finest batsmen ever produced from South African cricket—Faulkner, Nourse, Gordon White, J. H. Sinclair, Tancred, and so on. There were also D. L. A. Jephson and Walter Humphreys, each with only half of Simpson-Hayward's tricks; and they had their moments of mastery with underarms on 'modern' wickets against batsmen, not inferior to say the least, to to-day's. So it is a fair inference that if they were suddenly whisked to Broad-Halfpenny Down, there to defend wicket and shinbones against 'Lumpy' at the base of the brow of a hill, one or two of our contemporary heroes would find themselves like Bottom, terribly 'translated !' It is certain that on the rough turf of the heyday of the round-arm attack, they would appreciate the emotions of the poor cricketer named Ludd, who was struck on the foot by John Jackson, a giant in Nottinghamshire before Larwood, 1856-1862 to be precise. Poor Ludd hobbled in agony while Jackson appealed for 'leg-before.' And when the umpire announced 'Not hout!' Master Ludd said, 'Mebbe not, but I'm a-goin'.' John Jackson scaled fifteen stone and he measured six feet in his socks. He once lamented that he never achieved the distinction of taking all ten wickets in one innings but he brightened when he remembered that once, 'playin' for North against South, Ah bowled out nine of them and lamed Johnny Wisden so's he couldn't bat, which was just as good wasn't it?'

WE MIGHT CONJECTURE WITHOUT TOO MUCH fancifulness that the advent of the fast 'round-arm' attack hastened the passing of the tall hat which superseded the pretty three-cornered hat worn at Hambledon when the game was called 'elegant and manly.' The first All England XI sported the topper; its stately balance no doubt suited the tall forward style of Fuller Pilch, whom though he was a right-handed batsman, born in Norfolk, I shall take leave to describe as the Woolley of Kent cricket of the years 1835-1855. He mastered the round-arm cannonade even on turf so

Four Surrey Cricketers 1852
T. Sherman, Julius Caesar, W. Caffyn, T. Lockyer

rudely close to nature that at the beginning of one match he felt obliged to borrow a scythe and mow the grass a little smoother. Not until 1849 was it legal to sweep or roll the pitch between innings; and even then it was prepared in the simplest way, and the roller was probably no heavier than the one we use nowadays for the garden lawn. Bats were without 'humps'; the blade was of uniform thickness—or thinness—and there was no 'sprung' handle; in fact the whole bat, handle and blade, was cut out of one piece of wood. Much physical pain and nervous shock was presumably sustained by the batsman who 'came down' hard on a 'shooter,' or drove a fast ball with the bottom of the bat. The first cane-handle was an innovation of 1853. Pads, unknown to Hambledon, were experimented with round about 1836; then the onslaught on shins by the new fast bowlers quickened Mother Invention sharply and in the sixties pads and gloves became a necessary fashion, both of them almost apologetically frail, not at all a first line of offence, as the modern hardy warriors of Lancashire and Yorkshire wear *their* pads.

The danger of severe physical hurt has almost passed from first-class cricket. Even when Larwood bowled the body-line attack, so called, nobody was killed, or critically injured; and the danger was palpable with notice given open and unashamed. But the perils faced by batsmen on the crude turf of the older times against fast bowling—and it *was* fast—could not be anticipated; they came without warning; the best length ball might at any moment fly upward and knock a man out. Richard Daft, the Nottinghamshire classic, tells of the accident to young George Summers at Lord's. 'We were playing Notts. *v.* the M. C. C., and Platt was bowling at a terrific pace that season. Summers and Bignall were batting in our second innings, and the former, before he had scored, was struck on the cheek bone by a rising ball from Platt, and was carried off the field insensible. The blow caused concussion of the brain, and the poor fellow died three days afterwards.'

As early in the history of fast round-arm as Alfred Mynn, he was once so severely damaged on the leg during a long innings that he could scarcely stand; at last he was obliged to retire when, narrates Daft, 'his leg was found to be dreadfully injured. He was con-fined to his bed for a long period, and it was thought his surgeon would be obliged to take the leg off; but happily this extreme measure was not resorted to, and Mr. Mynn was afterwards quite sound again.' Mynn was born in 1807, a yeoman of Kent who, from early manhood until a few years before his death in 1861, was the first universally acknowledged of cricket's 'champions.' In his heyday he stood six feet one inch high; and he weighed nearly twenty stone but, vows Daft, there was nothing clumsy about his movements;

ALFRED MYNN 1852
'Stately and dignified at all times.'

they were, on the contrary, 'stately and dignified at all times.' He was the first really great fast round-arm bowler (in a tall hat) and there is strong evidence that he could pitch the ball on the leg stump and break to the off. When he died at the early age of fifty-four, he was immortalised—not by the statistics of his batting and bowling; no, he was remembered for his 'brave heart,' 'ever warm.' Some verses appeared in Bell's *Life* signed W. J. Prowse; and the closing stanza made a cadence of true poetry:

> With his tall and stately presence, with his nobly moulded form,
> His broad hand was ever open, his brave heart was ever warm.
> All were proud of him, all loved him. As the changing seasons pass,
> As our champion lies a-sleeping underneath the Kentish grass,
> Proudly, sadly, we will name him—to forget him were a sin—
> Lightly lie the turf upon thee, kind and manly Alfred Mynn.

No other game could inspire such a requiem for one of its players. There is scope at cricket for men to reveal themselves. For hours they are gathered together; and the ball is not flying here and there, leaving no time

26

for ayes and noes or any other revealing conversation or exchange of spirit. Between overs, at the fall of a wicket, in the slips while the fast bowler is walking back to his starting place—there is opportunity for human nature to 'come out strong.' And all the time the crowd sits around, and the players seem oblivious that they are being scrutinised, even though often the rhythm and procedure of cricket renders them as much exposed as actors on the stage. In truth when we look over the 'changing seasons' and remember them, we don't dwell on the records, the scores, the results; we see and savour again the men, the originals, the characters, all sorts and conditions, in a cavalcade of English character that travels slowly down the years from the meadows of Broad-Halfpenny to Lord's in June, with London spread outside, and the place full and the time of day just after the tea interval; and the Australians are beginning an innings in a Test match, and the crowd is assembled from the East and West Ends, not only of London, but of the Empire. 'Buses are running from the Bank to Mandalay. The Tavern is noisy and vernacular—Phil May and Belcher and Strube; and the Pavilion is a chapter out of Galsworthy: Jolyon, Soames and Dartie; and here are sallow-skinned men home from God knows what sweltering corners of the earth, their leave dwindling intolerably; and also you will catch a glimpse of turban and lovely silk purple shawl, or of white teeth flashing in black ivory, perhaps even of a fez and gold spectacles. Then suddenly, the call of 'Coo-ee!' comes from the enclosure under the clock, where Father Time with his scythe and wicket sways at the top in the breeze, a symbol of the game and of the summers that run away year by year like sand in the glass.

THIS IS THE MECCA OF CRICKET, AND WHEREVER A lover of the game may be he should turn his thoughts towards Lord's at the end of a summer day–at half past six possibly, when the deep velvet shadow has been thrown by the pavilion across the grass, and the last ball has been bowled, and the players are coming from the field, and the ground boys are putting the ropes round the pitch, while a few of the crowd group themselves in silent wonder as they look at the bruised earth where until a minute ago their heroes thundered away with fast off-breaks and square cuts. The long day's end . . . yet there is never any one moment at Lord's at close of play when you can say that the crowd has gone home; for long after a general vacancy has come over the scene, and long after the seats and the enclosures and the Mound stand have become depopulated, and long after the last flash of white flannels has vanished, and even after the solitary writer high up in the Press Box, more dilatory than his colleagues, has departed, one or two intimate figures will be seen sitting in the westering sunshine, reluctant to return to the world. And in the stately Long Room, the old historical pictures hang on the walls like mirrors that have not only reflected but captured and fixed into eternal attitudes all the cricketers and cricket matches that have ever been looked at through the pavilion's great windows; and even already the game that we have watched this very afternoon is mingling with the accumulated store of all the cricket Lord's has ever seen.

Lord's is a perfect name for the place—derived you might suppose from the fact that here is the High Court of cricket's legislature, here is sometimes a vintage aristocracy, and precedence and privilege, where even the tulips in the flower beds sport the M. C. C. colours. But no; Lord's might easily have been Brown's or even Wilkinson's. For it took its name from one Thomas Lord who rented a plot of land for cricket when the game became popular in London. First he built a ground where Dorset Square is now situated; then he carted the turf to St. John's Wood because the Portman family put up the rent. But not yet did Lord's settle down. The Regent Canal was designed to go straight through Lord's second venture, so once more, in 1814, he removed the turf, this time to the Lord's we all know and love to-day and for as long as life shall hold out.

LORD'S CRICKET GROUND 1837
Detail from a design printed on a silk handkerchief

There was another crisis, though. In 1825 Lord was losing money and he virtually decided to exploit the ground as a building estate. William Ward, Director of the Bank of England, thereupon asked what 'Lord's' was worth. 'Five thousand, sir,' was the answer, and there and then Ward signed a cheque for the amount and gave it to Lord. The donor had reason to cherish the ground; in 1820 he had batted there for the M.C.C. against Norfolk and had made 278 in a single innings—an individual score which was not beaten at Lord's until Holmes of Yorkshire amassed 315 not out against Middlesex more than a century later. Lord's first venture dates from May, 1787, some two years before the storming of the Bastille. Before the eighteenth century's close, Lord's had acquired its symbolical name and had attained an authority which has only been rendered more sacrosanct by the passing of every subsequent year. A Test match played elsewhere than at Lord's may be great and exciting and historical enough—and frequently it is; but whoever has not watched England and Australia at Lord's is in the position of the lover of the theatre who has seen Irving and Ellen Terry on tour at, say, Birmingham or Leeds. It is indeed a shattering thought—instead of Thomas Lord it could even have been the husband of Mrs. Tadgers.

If he had himself played the game skilfully we might well have imagined that Lord, like 'Lumpy,' got up early one morning and selected his pitch 'o'er a brow'; for a myriad of batsmen has been bowled neck-and-crop at Lord's by the ball that comes down the hill. Then the carting of Lord's original turf three times from place to place no doubt contributed to the imp of unease for ever afterwards resident in the turf at Lord's, where it is seldom a paradise for run-makers; moreover it is constantly in use from May to August, not only for the great (or greater) games but for those Homeric struggles between the Elevens of Clergy ('Band if possible'). One of these engagements (with a bishop behind the stumps) took place on a pitch rolled out about thirty yards from one roped off and almost ready for a Test match later in the week. And whenever a hit by some reverend Hobbs travelled across this Test match wicket, the fieldsman, with a proper religious observance, ran round it and never across it...

But it is not true that all pitches in the fast-round-arm epoch were rough and dangerous. Good batsmen needed only to play well at the Oval or Trent Bridge or Fenner's to have justice done to merit. If all wickets had behaved brutishly compelling blind reflex-action in the face of bowling which now kicked high and then shot to the stumps' base—in such circumstances there would have been no stylists amongst stroke-players, no Fuller Pilch and no (to come to the period of the authentic round-arm attack) Richard Daft, no

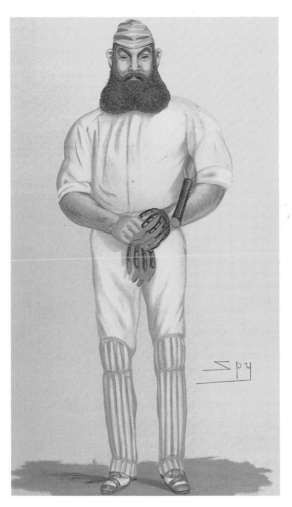

W. G. GRACE 1877

"The greatest of the Kings of cricket by natural-born right."

F. R. SPOFFORTH
"A terrific personal force possessed him."

Hayward (Thomas the First, in the sixties as renowned as his nephew in Surrey's heydey), no Caffyn, and George Parr—here were the players who fashioned the modern technique; they orchestrated the original folk-lore; they were the pioneers who tilled the field that gave us—soon after they had to go—the greatest batsmen the game has so far produced.

We can get some idea of the immense skill of the cricketers of the fifties and sixties if we remind ourselves that the bowler's arm was not allowed to rise above the shoulder in delivery until 1835, and not until 1862 was the over-arm action legalised. Yet by the time we come to the seventies—measured in duration of cricket seasons, a mere two or three years—W. G. Grace has been harvested; the incomparable A. G. Steel, and Alfred Shaw, one of the greatest of slow-medium bowlers; and Tom Emmett with his spin from leg stump to off bail, which he called the sostenuter'; and R. F. Miles, slow left-hand, the first off-theorist; and Alec Watson of Lancashire, slow to medium; and I. D. Walker, noted for brilliant hits past cover. Before we reach 1880, Spofforth has been evolved, and now the game is so modern in its main technical foundations that we may doubt whether any contemporary XI would be good enough to defeat the best XI chosen from the years 1870-1880. This great blossoming could not have happened if the cricketers of the middle ages had not fertilised the game with skill of potentiality and of permanent influence.

First-class cricket of the years now under discussion was dominated by the All England XI which toured England from early summer until late September, and played against odds. County cricket had to wait a little longer for organisation, though Sussex, the oldest of all County clubs, played Nottinghamshire at Nottingham on September 7th and 8th in 1835, and lost by three wickets, in the absence of Lillywhite be it remembered! One of the immortals of Sussex cricket is, of course, John Wisden, who was five feet four inches in height and weighed seven stone in his early days, and bowled fast—and easily—and took 2,707 wickets between the years of 1848 and 1859. But his name lives best in the mellowing colour of his 'Almanack,' that granary of the game's seasonal yield.

An event of some historical peculiarity occurred in 1859 when the All England XI, all professionals, crossed the Atlantic to play five matches in Canada and America. They won them all, even though one of them was interrupted by a snowstorm; the team did not leave England before September 7th, and the mid-October weather at Rochester was severe. George Parr was captain, and his colleagues were Carpenter, Caffyn, Lockyer, Grundy, Hayward, Wisden, Diver,

Stephenson, Lillywhite, John Jackson and Julius Caesar—yes, that was his name, by Christian baptism, and he was born at Godalming, and a little man and very fierce with his bat, and quick of eye and feet. There is a celebrated photograph of this first of all voyaging England XIs, taken on board ship; they are decoratively grouped, with the rigging and the scuppers and other nautical paraphernalia about them. Nearly all of them wear whiskers growing round and under the chin of clean-shaven faces; also they wear striped or spotted shirts, and caps of the Bill Sykes fashion. Altogether they present the aspect of the crew of the 'Jolly Roger'; and Wisden is the image of Smee—Captain Hook's amiable cut-throat colleague. There is one exception—George Parr the captain looks like a notable evangelist of the period.

The game was out of its nonage at last. The limbs and the muscles were ready, stretched free and ardent; the field was open and fertile. The hour was ripe for the coming of age; in homelier language, the time had arrived for cricket to be 'put on the map' once and for all. Of course, the moment produced the man, the living symbol and apotheosis (though no doubt he would stroke his beard at the sound of such language and wonder what it was all about).

He was born in 1848 and he learned to play in an orchard in a village near Bristol. His father was a country doctor, so crazy about cricket that he would rise at dawn to play in the nets. The mother, too, understood the game. And he had an elder brother called 'The Coroner.'

It was the Bach family all over again, now born to a game. There was 'G. F.' famous as a stylish and prolific batsman; there was 'Fred,' who died young and was a marvellous catcher. The crack of the bat coming over the meadow and the barking of a dog who was a happy field, tongue hanging out, ready on taut defiant forelegs as the next ball was being bowled—these were the sounds heard by the labourer as he went to his work in the fresh of spring-time mornings. 'The Gra-aces pla-ayin' at cricket,' he probably said to himself. But he could scarcely have guessed that in this adjacent orchard an eminent Victorian was being made, soon to be renowned everywhere and for ever after as 'W. G.'

He played his first county match at the age of fourteen in August, 1862, and scored 18 out of 92. Next year against Somersetshire, he scored 52 not out and took six wickets for 43. In 1864 he was chosen as substitute for his brother, E. M. (who was absent playing in Australia), in a match against the Gentlemen of Sussex at the Oval. The boy of 16 batted first wicket down and scored 170, and next innings was unbeaten for 52. At the age of 18 he amassed 224 not out for England *v.* Surrey, then asked his Captain for temporary leave from the match while he dashed away to the Crystal Palace to win a quarter-mile hurdle race. Though he himself stated that he came to mastery only by severe practice and perseverance, it is difficult not to go on thinking that he entered the field fully armed—Jove out of Minerva. Portraits taken of him while he was still in his teens reveal him already bearded like the pard. But he was lean and angular then.

His career had the Victorian longitude, opulence, and regnancy. To this day, when his records have been surpassed by the Hammonds and Bradmans and Ponsfords, he still dwarfs them; he is a happy easeful Atlas holding up in his hand, but as though it were a cricket ball, the world in which they enjoy their brief statistical day; for 'W. G.' invented them, so to say; he created the conditions under which they came into existence at all. Here we must quote the finest of all summings-up of his contribution, from Ranjit-sinhji's *Jubilee Book* (but I cannot attribute it to 'Ranji' himself; possibly it was Fry's or Case's inspiration): 'He revolutionised cricket. He turned it from an accomplishment into a science; he united in his mighty self all the good points of all the good players and made utility the criterion of style...; he turned the old one-stringed instrument into a many-chorded lyre.'

More than that; cricket's genius, its Englishness of nature, became visible and incarnate in him; he was

The Harbor at Cork

King of Cricket by born right, and he looked it every inch, every ounce, never incongruous on the sward even in his last years of benignly accumulating flesh and greying beard. But it must never be forgotten that at his high noon he was a superb example of manhood, every muscle quick in him, no superfluity, his brow classical and his eyes keen and fine. He was s a boy when the round-arm bowling changed to overarm; which means he had to counter a species of attack different from that by which so far his skill had been practised. Apparently he noticed no difference, for the solemn truth is that in a few seasons he smashed fast bowling, discredited it, or to use the stronger and more appropriate word from Charles Dickens, 'spifflicated' it. There were, of course, other causes of this temporary loss of faith in sheer pace. Wickets were now more reliably prepared on the whole; Alfred Shaw expounded the virtue of length; none the less the spur to ideas and strategy came mainly from the Champion, who organised back-play to forward-play into one; before Grace, players had used one or the other method, seldom the two in instinctive combination.

The bare figures of his performances in first-class cricket are these: he played from 1862 to 1908 and scored 54,896 runs in 1,388 innings, average 39.55. He took 2,864 wickets at 17.97 each. In 1871, he scored 2,739 runs in the season, average 78. The next best batsman of that year was Daft with not half the average. Here is the difference in the majesty of 'W. G.' in those days and the *réclame* of the modern heroes. He was high above the general best. Bradman might achieve his average of 80; but somebody will be on his heels; there will be a dozen at least not far behind. When 'W. G' 'failed' it was as though some hitch had gone wrong in natural law. Year after year his reign burgeoned, season upon season, like the surge and sequence of a symphony of cricket.

At last it seemed the cadence was about to fall. Forty years was considered a good age for anybody then; and 'W. G.' began to recede from the pinnacles to the ordinary flat lands of good honest cricketers. The public took him more and more to their hearts: a Grand Old Man ready for his Nunc Dimittis! In 1895 he was in his forty-seventh year. To the pride and joy of all, with bowlers mingling apprehension and bewilderment with these nobler emotions, 'W. G.' compiled one thousand runs in May. He opened with 13 and 103 for M. C. C. and Sussex, followed by insignificant innings against Yorkshire. Next he made 288 *v.* Somerset (his 100th century); and after 50 or so *v.* Cambridge University, he came to Gravesend. Kent batted first and Grace fielded while they piled up 470, and went in first for Gloucestershire and was tenth out for 257, then after Kent had been put out for 76, he hit off in an hour 73 of the 103 needed for a great victory, with a quarter of an hour to spare. He was on the field from beginning to end of the match, every ball. On the 30th, he needed 153 to complete a thousand runs in May—a feat not only unprecedented but not dreamed of. He won the toss against Middlesex; and of course the luck with the spin of the coin was all he needed. A magnum of champagne, drunk in mid-wicket, celebrated the event; and in accordance with the eternal fitness of things, the scene was Lord's.

Grace was a Representative Man of his epoch; the crowds flocked to look upon him—and thus he changed cricket to a national affair, a spectacle as well as a game; and with his coming, the counties lived on him and increased. If he wasn't at the wicket, he was on view just the same—bowling or fielding with heart and soul and shrewdness. He bowled high-tossed leg-breaks which did not always break. He would run to the wicket, elbows out, huge yellow cap on his head, whiskers blowing in the wind, and he would turn his wrist and emit a grunt indicative of a terrible spin; and the ball would go straight through the air, inviting a mighty hit to leg—where 'W. G.' always had a man ready near the boundary. He 'diddled' hundreds of victims out that way. One afternoon, though, a young cricketer fresh from the University went in to bat against Gloucestershire, and declined to walk into 'W. G.'s trap.

The young man did not see why he should be so foolish, so instead of hitting the Old Man's slows to long-leg's clutches, he merely tapped them safely to the ground for ones and twos. 'W. G.' continued for a few overs, grunting and twisting, and still the young man tapped the full tosses for safe singles and twos round the corner, until 'W. G.' came down the pitch and cried out :

'Looky here, young feller, if you keep on doing that I'll take myself off I will, I'll take myself off.'

There were others like him, or at any rate of the same stock and vintage—A. N. Hornby for example, who followed hounds in the winter and broke any amount of ribs, and in the summer came hallooing into the field like Squire Western, red in the face and jubilant and blasphemous in sudden turn, either running Barlow to death from short singles, maybe skying the ball in mid-wicket and shouting 'Come two—they'll miss it!' Hornby once told me that 'W. G.' at times was compelled to take severe measures when a batsman defied all legal ways and means of getting him out. On such occasions he would slyly make a sign to first-slip, and first-slip would creep silently behind the wicket to short fine-leg, where the unsuspecting batsman would discover himself unexpectedly caught, the bowler having supplied the right ball by arrangement. Hornby and the Lancashire amateurs decided to hoist 'W. G.' by his own petard. At Bristol he was well set for his century;

and while he stood erect facing Johnny Briggs, bat lifted, toe cocked upward, A. N. Hornby signalled to first-slip, who even as the bowler was more than halfway through his run stole across to fine-leg. He was nearly there when the Old Man cried out, in his high-pitched voice 'I can see what you're doin'—I can see what yer doin'.'

We have the authority of A. C. M. Croome for believing that Grace 'never moved his feet, like Ranjitsinhji,' and never 'used the back-stroke in the modern style.' From this statement I take it that 'W. G.' on fast wickets mainly played forward, from a back foot used as a sort of stanchion; and played defensively by moving the right foot backwards but not across the stumps; in other words, he did not 'cover' with his pads. In the old photos we can admire the defensive play of the masters, poised sometimes entirely on the right foot, left leg almost prancing upward, bat straight as a die, the three wickets exposed to all the breakbacks in the world. On the face of it, the bowler's task was easy then compared with the modern problem; at any rate once the bat was beaten the bowler usually got his reward. There was no canny 'second line' of pads to frustrate him, after all. But the probability is that excessive leg-play has given more wickets away cheaply to the modern bowlers than all the lapses of technique of which 'W. G.' and Daft and Shrewsbury and all the classics were guilty.

Even in a mere game, though, nothing is new under the sun. It is generally supposed that 'Ranji' was the first batsman to discredit the old principle of the firm right foot, and instead, to put into force the doctrine: 'Find out where the ball is. Go there. Hit it.' Nyren tells of Fennex of Hambledon, the 'first who went in laid into a ball before it had time to rise.' And Billy Beldham himself scared Squire Powlett almost to death—'You do frighten me there jumping out of your ground!' An old Nottinghamshire player who dropped much sweat into the grass bowling at the Old Man offen spoke to me of 'W. G.'s footwork; but apparently he forgot to emphasise its deficiencies: 'His big body med th' wickets look so little that you felt ball weren't big enough. And 'e kept puttin' 'is right leg half-way down the pitch smotherin' t' spin, and hey! I sometimes felt weak as mi grandmother!' Genius has a habit of devising ways and means of its own. Rigid right foot or no, it is the fact that 'W.G.' usually found where the ball was—we have the word of a minister of the Gospels for it. The Rev. A. P. Wickham was wicket-keeper for Somersetshire when 'W. G.' scored 288 at Bristol in May, 1895, and he noticed from his position behind the stumps that 'W. G.' in all that colossal innings allowed four balls, and four only, to pass his bat.

Only one riddle of bowling really baffled Grace, and he was nearly sixty years old then. The 'googly,' virtually unknown until he had passed his fiftieth year, put him more or less out of countenance. But does anybody doubt that in his prime he would not have knocked the 'googly' severely on the head, with all other dodges and last resorts of bowlers? 'I pitches the ball where I likes,' said J. C. Shaw, master of his craft in the sixties and the seventies, 'but that b—,' meaning 'W. G.,' ' 'e puts it where 'e likes.'

He grew in the high noon of cricket's history. For nearly half a century the springtime came round for him, and he went out and trod the fresh grass; the elements of sun and air and wind and summer rain became part of him. Year succeeded year; he piled them up behind him like his vast runs, until one April day he played at Kennington Oval in 1908. It was bleak and cold; winter had hung on bitterly that year. Snow blew in the wind, and some flakes fell on the Old Man's whitening beard.

H E NEVER PLAYED AGAIN ON A GREAT CRICKET field; this was his end as the greatest of the Kings of cricket by natural-born right. He was the arch over which the a game advanced out of a dim legendary past into authentic and contemporary history. To cope with 'W.G.'—and sometimes to avoid having to cope with

45

THE DRAW
From a series of batting cartoons, 1845

him—the off-theory length bowlers came into being; they pitched wide of the stumps and packed the field to the off. It was an evasion, for the most part, and of little permanent value as a spectacle or a match-winning device. We do not belittle Alfred Shaw if we decline to-day to count him amongst the really creative geniuses amongst bowlers. His was a triumph of perseverance and precision; in his career he bowled 24,700 overs, and nearly 17,000 of them were maidens. It was the period of thrift and of Samuel Smiles—cricket has usually (as we shall see, as we proceed with our story) reflected changes in the national ways of thought and conduct. Length, length, length! First principles and not much imagination. 'W. G.' saw further than that; when his career began he bowled in the general fashion—medium-paced and pretty straight-forward, his chief ally the unruly turf. But he learned, not only from his own experience but from the example of another forgotten pioneer who saw with the vision of poetic opportunism that there was no future, on grounds that year after year more and more favoured the batsman, no future at all for length by mechanical rotation. David Buchanan was originally a fast left-hander, and he changed in the late sixties to slow spin, and in ten matches for the Gentlemen *v.* the Players, from 1868 to 1874, he took 87 wickets for less than 15 runs each. Grace then tried his new dodge; he trusted to well-tossed slows, pitched on the leg-stump, with a bias away from the bat. We have lived to take it as a major axiom that no bowler on a heavily rolled wicket can hope to be counted amongst the really great unless he uses the air, and spins or veers not in *to* the bat but away from it, seeking the edge. 'W. G.' probably never turned the ball as viciously or as abruptly as his wrist contortions and stomach grunts were confidently intended to suggest; none the less the root of the matter was in him. He would have chuckled to see 'Clarrie' Grimmett, who only yesterday was a devastating 'modern' exploiter of spin and flight with an arm probably seldom as high as the Old Man's. The history of cricket is one long battle of wits between batsman and bowler, the groundsman holding the ring. After the physical-force assaults of Jackson and Willsher came the Fabian economy of off-theory. But the time was ripening at last for the first authentic modern bowler. The problem was here for him to solve—'W.G.' on a reasonably good wicket. The materials of a scientific and sophisticated attack were waiting for him: length, flight, various kinds of pace and spin, though as yet they were distributed amongst many exponents; no one man commanded them all. Whoever should arrive at this psychological moment and assemble in a single comprehensive and beautifully graded craft the scattered but deadly elements would be hailed as the first of the great bowlers of 'modern' cricket.

And he came most carefully upon his hour. Moreover he came a considerable distance, all the way from Australia in fact. His name was Spofforth.

Iᴺ 1861 ᴀɴᴏᴛʜᴇʀ Eɴɢʟɪsʜ ᴄʀɪᴄᴋᴇᴛ ᴛᴇᴀᴍ ᴠᴏʏᴀɢᴇᴅ overseas, this time as far as Australia, known metaphorically as 'Down Under,' and supposedly inhabited mainly by Ned Kelly and his band. Spiers and Pond managed the venture, and the players, all professional, were guaranteed £150 and expenses. The ship unobtrusively left Liverpool on October 18, and was never heard of again until it arrived at Melbourne on Christmas Eve, where it might easily have been met on the quay by Mr. Micawber. To-day when we send a Test match team to Australia in a floating hotel we can learn by wireless from hour to hour where they are and of the state of their health; but in case of accidents we send an army of them, with adequate reserves or rein-forcements. No more than twelve men comprised this first English team to Australia in 1861, and their names were H. H. Stephenson, Caffyn, Griffith, Mortlock, Mudie, Sewall, Lawrence, Bennett, Hearne, Wells, Iddison and E. Stephenson. It was an Australian summer of terrific heat in an age of no air-conditioning and no refrigerators. The travellers were much impressed by the Melbourne Cricket Ground, which boasted not

only a handsome pavilion and a grandstand but its own supply of water. A dozen matches were played, all against odds. Six were won, four drawn, and two lost. All the players returned safely home, excepting Lawrence, who accepted an engagement as coach, the first of the sowers of a perennial harvest. A second team landed in Australia in 1864; it included the great Caffyn, who like Lawrence, stayed behind as coach. In 1868 a team of Aboriginals braved the rigours of seafaring and an English summer; and in 1873 'W. G.' himself took out the third English team and had his leg-stump knocked back in the first match of the season by H. F. Boyle. Three years afterwards witnessed the beginning of recognisedly historical Test matches; and England actually tasted defeat at Melbourne on March 17, 1877.

Nothing could satisfy the avid Australians now, and they invaded England in the freezing May of 1878 and suffered reverse and incipient pneumonia at Nottingham, their first engagement. They came to Lord's on May 27, and most people in London expected them to be as the Aboriginals all over again. This day proved the most momentous in cricket's annals. The Australians were opposed by the M. C. C., and at noon W. G. Grace and A. N. Hornby began batting against the attack of Allan and Boyle. Grace struck the first ball of the match for four and was caught at square-leg off the second. The score was twenty for one wicket when a tall man, with legs and arms that worked with a ramrod sort of action, somehow reminiscent of one of the earliest 'rocket' engines, bowled instead of Allan. He at once staggered Lord's as never before or since; he went through the M. C. C. innings like a storm; and took six wickets for four runs in twenty-three balls. This was Spofforth.

The M. C. C. lost a low-scoring match by nine wickets; Grace in the second innings was missed at the wicket before he had scored, off Spofforth, and was clean bowled next ball. H. S. Altham, most accurate of the game's historians, records that the Australians' victory over the M. C. C. 'was a nine-day wonder.' It was probably the most notable and famous of all cricket victories. For consider: Grace in the seventies stood for invincibility. 'W. G.' and ten others usually meant an easy overwhelming of the next best XI in England. Not much imagination is needed to realise the magnitude of the Australian conquest at Lord's on that showery morning of May 27, 1878, accomplished by players of a country 'beyond the pale,' with a population far below London's, not to say Lancashire's. Other English cricketers overwhelmed with Grace and Hornby in this match were Alfred Shaw, Morley, A. J. Webbe, Flowers—a nucleus which in conditions obtaining in the seventies would, I think, prove a safeguard against defeats at the hands of any English team chosen from any period, from Hambledon to the present day.

In 1880, the first Test match on English soil was played at Kennington Oval, arranged at the last minute of an Australian tour so diffidently entered into that at one part of the summer the Australians advertised in the newspapers their readiness to play anywhere or anybody. The date of this great match was September 6, 7 and 8; and it was necessary to recall our finest amateur talent from the moors and shooting boxes of Scotland. 'W. G.' scored 152, and England were 420 all out; to which Australia answered with only 149 and following on 271 behind, lost six for 170 by close of play on the second afternoon, and then—prophetic of things to come and of the Australian disbelief in lost causes—the last two men helped W. L. Murdoch, the captain, to add 140; and Murdoch, later to become bosom-friend of 'W.G.' and to go in first with him in many a London County innings at the Crystal Palace, was undefeated for 153. England, wanting only 57 to win, lost five wickets for twenty, and it needed 'W. G.' and Frank Penn to pull the game through.

The writing was so luridly aflame on the wall that only a certain passage of time could now stand between the threat of the wrath to come and the fulfilment. And in late August, 1882, again at Kennington Oval,

Australia won against England for the first time in England—by 8 runs—and so laid claim to an equality of prowess in cricket with our best once and for all and ever after. It was a match all over within two days, the 28th and 29th of the month in a rainy period. Murdoch won the toss against the English captain Hornby; and shortly after three o'clock the Australians were 64 all out. Spofforth then 'shattered' 'W. G.'s wickets for four, and at close of play England were all out too, and only 38 in front. There was more heavy rain in the night, and next morning the pitch was so drenched that the ball was like a cake of soap and the grounds-man was obliged to use a spade to clear away the mud. On the easy dead turf, Australia seized her chance with the opportunism of her breed. Bannerman stonewalled while Hugh Massie hurled his bat at everything and made 55 out of 66 in as many minutes before he was bowled, first wicket down, by A. G. Steel. But the English bowlers here got on top; Peate with his left-handed 'floaters.' Australia could get no more than 56 for nine, after Massie left, and England wanted only 85 to win.

In the Australian dressing-room between innings, Spofforth quietly said: 'Boys, this thing can be done.' The tale has often been told. . . . an autumn afternoon was going to its fall in a grey light when Hornby and Grace went to the wicket to face Spofforth and

54

Garrett. The crowd filled the ground and was so silent that the tinkling of a hansom-cab could be heard coming closer along the Vauxhall Road.' Spofforth bowled Hornby when England had reached 15; but Grace and George Ulyett of Yorkshire virtually settled the matter by taking the total to 51. And now Spofforth changed ends and attacked with the pavilion behind him, and got Ulyett caught at the wicket immediately.

Two runs later Grace was out trying to drive Boyle. With the game and everybody in a purgatory, 12 successive maiden overs were bowled. A hit was then wilfully bungled to allow Spofforth to 'get at' Lyttleton, who succumbed forthwith to a brutal break-back.

When Peate, also of Yorkshire, went in last, England needed 10, and Studd was at the other end. Peate, a great bowler, was without a vestige of organised batsmanship. It is doubtful whether he ever possessed a bat of his own; anything lying about the dressing-room would do, an old table-leg. He hit his first ball, a slow from Boyle, for two, and was bowled by his third; and Studd could only look on helpless. It is alleged that Peate, when asked 'Why, man, didn't you just stop them; why did you try to hit?' replied: 'Hey, but Ah just couldn't trust Maister Studd, beggin' yer pardon.'

During the closing half-hour of this famous victory and downfall, the excitement at Kennington Oval was so intense that one spectator dropped down dead, and another, after all was over, was surprised to discover that he had bitten large and irreplaceable pieces out of his umbrella-handle.

THE AUSTRALIANS BROUGHT TO OUR VICTORIAN pastime a terrible realism and cunning. After all, there had been in the vigour and wit of Grace and Hornby and the other squires and yeomen a certain overgrown schoolboy gusto and licence at times to jape and play the fool. But these Australians were cricketers who had come quickly to rare skill in a country with no cant at all in sport, no 'traditions' and what not. They were not hampered by old custom; during the English tour of 1876–77 the Englishmen had to bat on a rough wicket at Sydney and next day the Australians rolled and heavily watered a new pitch for *their* first innings. As time went on they conformed to a more equitable legality; but they continued to see things with fresh eyes, and allowed no stiffening of technical or strategical procedure through precedence. They set different positions in field. During a period when the slow of foot and the unsure of finger were hidden away at square-leg and mid-on, the Australians made these positions hostile and important. On 'sticky' wickets mid-on intimidated the batsman only seven yards away from the bat. Absit omen!—or (once again) Mene, Mene,

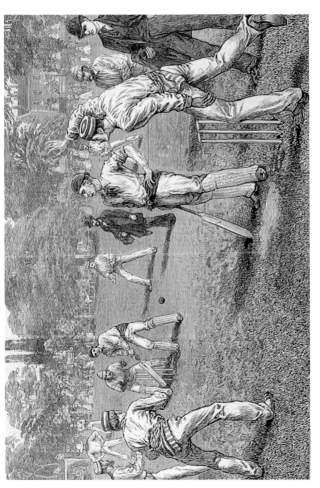

THE AUSTRALIANS *V.* THORTON'S XI AT ORLEANS HOUSE –
SPOFFORTH BOWLING WALKER, 1878

Tekel, Upharsin. Blackham the wicket-keeper dispensed with a long-stop. This embryo leg-trap snapped-up catches sent by reflex-action from the breakbacks of Spofforth, who directed his attack on the off and middle stumps.

Spofforth was called the 'Demon' bowler when he bowled fast in 1878. But in 1882 he had changed his method. Lord Harris, who could speak from severe experience, has recorded that Spofforth was very fast before he came to England, 'but he soon found that on our softer wickets he could 'do' so much that, instead of bowling fast with an occasional 'judgment' ball, as he called it, he changed to bowling the medium-paced ball as a rule, with an occasional fast one, and so became one of the best bowlers ever seen; in my opinion the best I have ever played.'

Old men who knew him and experienced him on the field of play, agree that Spofforth's best ball broke back. Now the great ball of modern cricket, as we have seen, is the one that pitches on the leg-stump and 'whips away' towards the off, keeping close to the bat. Most contemporary cricketers will not doubt that the ball which 'leaves the bat' as it breaks away is more difficult to play than the off-break. There are known strokes which may be more or less trusted to counter the off-break (no matter under what l.b.w. rule); this ball comes inward to the bat and can be hit or pushed 'with the spin.' No stroke has yet been devised that can safely be exploited against the quick ball that breaks away after pitching on the 'blind' spot. That is why S. F. Barnes was probably a greater bowler technically than Spofforth. I have found no evidence that Spofforth 'ran' the ball away from the bat. But it is not possible to account for the prowess of Spofforth by an analysis of his technique. A terrific personal force possessed him—not so Barnes, who often was sulky and depressed or indifferent, an ordinary mortal visited by the moods of small men. A dynamo of hostility worked ceaselessly in Spofforth; he got on the nerves of his opponents; he had the evil eye; he was tall and angular and satanic of aspect. Spofforth was Australia's spearhead from 1878 to 1886; and it is significant that Australia won nine Test matches to England's eight from 1878 to 1886, then lost 10 out of 11. There were reasons other than cricket to account for the sudden eclipse; the Australians quarrelled in their own country between themselves. And too long they lagged behind in scientific batsmanship. There was the stone-waller, Bannerman, true; on the whole, there was an excess of offence and not enough defence. Two immortal bowlers kept the lustre aglow in the doldrum years, Turner and Ferris who in one English summer of 'sticky' pitches took together 534 wickets.

In 1891-1892, W. G. Grace again went to Australia,

captain of Lord Sheffield's team. Strong though his forces were, he had to bow to defeat in two out of three Test matches. Bannerman was the spinal column of Australia—three and three-quarters of an hour for 45; four hours for 41; and seven and a half hours for 91. And the beautiful hitter J. J. Lyons was there, too; this was the authentic Australian balance of obstinacy and aggression. By the time Australia celebrates in Test matches her 21st year, from 1878 to 1899, she has given to the game batsmen whose names are fit to be pronounced with any of ours: Giffen, Darling, Noble, Trumper, Hill, and Gregory, Armstrong, Trumble, Worrall, Saunders, Trott, and by the last of them I mean Albert, who was rejected by his own country and came to live in London, and played for Middlesex and seemed to become as permanent at Lord's and as necessary as the Tavern itself. He drove a ball over the pavilion, and devoted his remaining days as a batsman to attempts to repeat the stroke. He was one of the greatest artists in spin and flight and curving temptations of flight. He allowed imagination to possess him on the occasion of his benefit at Lord's; for he did the 'hat-trick' twice in the same innings and finished off the match before three days of gate money had been gathered; in an ecstasy of skill and genius he bowled himself into the bankruptcy court. Australians are usually shrewder than that; the truth is Albert Trott was changed by environment and love of London into a romantic Cockney. Like another and later cricketer, also an artist and a humorous experimenter with the possibilities of a disguised and sometimes open and palpable full-toss, Trott never fitted into the Australian canon; I refer to the incorrigible Arthur Mailey, who bowled slows like a millionaire, indifferent to the general competitive currency and rates of exchange.

There has always been a certain dourness about Australian cricket, an unashamed will-to-power, with no 'may the best side win' nonsense. Even the brilliant Victor Trumper was an Ironside in Cavalier's colours, his bat a conquering sword, not a lance in a tournament. There has never been an Australian Palairet or an Australian Woolley; the stylish Alan Kippax of— recent history came close to grace and refinement and absence of masculinity— and he was not appreciated in the Australian War Councils.

THE YEARS EXTENDING FROM 1890 TO 1914 witnessed the Golden Age of batsmanship. Years of sowing were now reaped: the technique was ready for cultured use. The stage was at last prepared; and the producer was the groundsman and his roller. A great batsman could now on fine days give his mind to the display of his arts, confident that he need only solve the known problems of his material—in other words

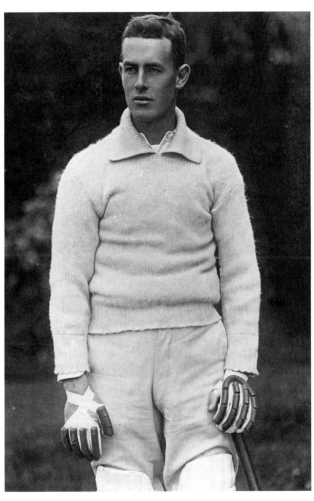

VICTOR TRUMPER
'An Ironside in Cavalier's colours, his bat a conquering sword.'

the bowling opposed to him, which could be studied in the abstract as well as in fact, free of incalculable and unscientific misconduct caused by a rough and entirely unscientific pitch. The groundsman, the producer or stage manager of cricket, made the mistake of producers in the theatre—he became engrossed—in the spectacle and the setting at the expense of the play. He made the conditions in which a virtuoso display of skill was positively encouraged; the great batsman could absorb himself in the perfection of his own art in the face of an attack largely reduced to a static mechanism. But there was scope also for the virtuoso bowler—for none except the inspired artist of pace or spin or flight could hope on a perfect pitch to emerge from a perspiring anonymity. The circumstances so much favoured batsmanship that the technique of stroke-play and footwork developed at a pace which outran and outwitted every bowler not of the highest class.

If the first modern bowler was Spofforth, the first modern batsman was Arthur Shrewsbury. He would find little to trouble his method in the latest contemporary attack; because he played back mainly and—what prescience and prophecy!—he covered up with his pads. According to my researches, he was the first systematically to use the 'second line of defence' and to base his defence on the back foot *close to the spinning ball*. He played forward only when he could safely reach to the

63

ball's pitch—unless the flight deceived him, which was seldom. Possibly his want of physical height and robustness contributed to his adoption of a technique which, if we could see him to-day, would not seem in the slightest old-fashioned, except that the style would have a dignity not of the present. Of all batsmen famous before 1890, he is the only one I can think of who would not seem a little archaic if we saw him at Lord's to-morrow, with Hutton at the other end. We might indeed imagine that Hutton was one of his disciples.

His influence on the future of batsmanship was as potent as Ranjitsinhji's at a later date. Shrewsbury demonstrated that the ball could be watched almost to the bat on the 'stickiest' wicket. He was, indeed, the greatest of all players on a 'sticky' wicket. In the second Test match of 1886, played at Lord's, he scored 164 on a pitch that changed from fiery to slow and to 'sticky'—and Spofforth was bowling at his best. In 1887, Shrewsbury's batting average was 78 with an aggregate of 1,653 runs. The next best batsman that year was 'W.G.,' with an average of 54. But Shrewsbury played many of his innings at Trent Bridge, usually a heaven for batsmen, with the turf a cushion stuffed with runs. The Nottinghamshire XI was renowned in the mid-eighties and early nineties for power and majesty of batsmanship; not a few of the

G. L. JESSOP 1901
"A scientific hitter, a scorer of runs by hurricane."

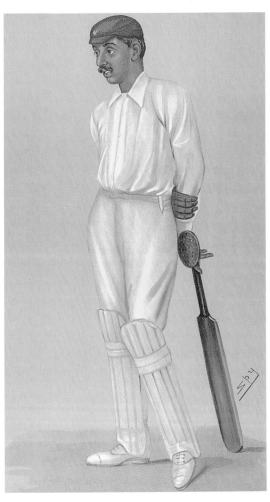

K. S. Ranjitsinhji 1897
"The most wonderful batsman of the lot,
inexplicable unless in terms of genius."

players succumbed to the temptation to regard stately motions of the bat as an end artistic and sufficient in itself. Scotton was the most notorious of all slow-scorers, his bat a closed door. And there was William Gunn, tall and elegant, yet strong, as patient as Shrewsbury, as watchful, as unmoved by common lapse of time. Shrewsbury and Gunn! Their names in conjunction were as familiar in the ears of boys of *their* epoch as ever Hobbs and Sutcliffe in theirs—and, we thought, as everlasting.

Batsmanship was now a thing in itself which the crowds flocked to see, apart from any particularly palpitating anxiety about the result of the match. One after another the procession increases as it moves across our sunset stage. Shrewsbury and Gunn and John Shuter and the Reads of Surrey; then the crescendo—Maclaren and Fry and Bobby Abel and Hayward and Palairet and Brown and Tunnicliffe and Quaife and Johnny Tyldesley and a host of others and also the Australians; but all of them, no matter how high they stood, overshadowed at last by the most wonderful batsman of the lot, inexplicable unless in terms of genius.

THE ARTS AND TECHNIQUE OF ALL THE GREAT players—excepting those of this wizard—can be explained as the effect of known causes; they grew out of

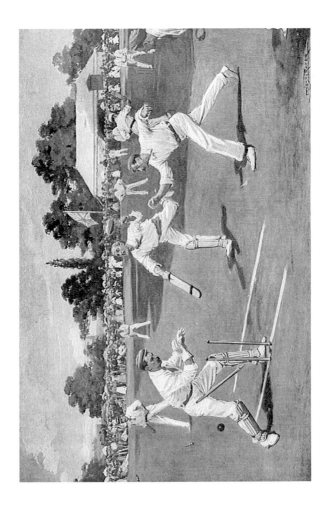

one another as the game developed by slow but natural
stages, with here and there a comprehensive summing-up
of known principles and a prophetic but logical antici-
pation of the next move forward. But now arrived a
batsman who was unique; he was not biologically
accountable; he was a case of a complete and magical
divergence from type. For though his method as a
whole could be related to the new school which departed
from classical forward play with a left foot thrust to the
ball's pitch from a grounded right foot; though he on
the contrary expounded the doctrine of the movable
right foot, his secret was not to be found here. Other
batsmen, contemporary with him, acted on his principle
of 'Find where the ball is and go to it.' This necro-
mancer did not ever seem to *have* to find where the ball
was; he magnetically drew it to him, surely, or charmed
it into that circle of magic flashing and rotating around
his supple wrists. He was as still as a slender tree when
the bowler released the ball—that is to say, his immo-
bility was only intensified by the lovely rippling of his
silk shirt, which apparently was rendered sensitive by
pulsations from his nerves and blood.

A fast breakback pitched in front of him, lightning
from Lockwood, and there was an exquisite movement,
a flick of the bat as the left foot gracefully crossed the
right, and lo! the ball was quivering and palpitatingly
on its way to the boundary, not just going there but as

though endowed with delighted and enchanted momentum.

He was a remarkable instance of the power and scope of cricket to express not only the style that is the man but also the style that is the race. The game was English through and through when he came to it, almost Victorian in fact; the straight bat and the length ball; first principles; or what might be called an ethically sanctioned technique, open and palpable and honoured by long respectable use. A strange light from the East flickered in the English sunshine when he was at the wicket; 'He's no batsman,' said the Australian George Giffen, 'he's a conjuror!' When he turned approved science upside down and changed the geometry of batsmanship to an esoteric legerdemain, we were bewitched to the realms of rope-dancers and snake-charmers; this was a cricket of Oriental sorcery, glowing with a dark beauty of its own, a beauty with its own mysterious axis and balance. Bowlers threw up their hands to high heaven as he made his passes of flexible willow and they saw their thunderbolts enchanted from the middle stump to the fine-leg boundary—it was like a shooting star, all wrong in our astronomy, but right and splendid in some other and more dazzling stellar universe. ' 'e never made a Christian stroke in 'is life,' said an old Yorkshire cricketer. And why should he have? His name was not

Grace but Kumar Shri Ranjitsinhji.

The Golden Age of batsmanship was based, like most ages of gold, on an aristocracy. This was the period of the amateur cricketer; even in the industrial North of England a noble Lord was leader of the Yorkshire XI; and there was also an 'Honourable' in the team—that same Yorkshire which in a later and more severely economic epoch was to become representative of canny Trade-Unionism, a team of wage-earners, 'pros,' with one unpaid and well-to-do as captain just to conform to social etiquette in general. In the nineties cricket was looked upon as the gentlemen's game; tennis was not yet popular with men of proper late-Victorian masculinity; it was a game for what was then known as the 'masher,' with his straw 'boater,' and his designs on the 'fair sex.' Golf was for the more than middle-aged; while football was deemed mainly 'low,' unless it was impossible to play for the Corinthians. From the public schools and the Universities, English cricket acquired characteristics of assurance, privilege and indifference to the crowd and the results, characteristics not to be found in the play of Australians or South Africans. What's bred in the bone comes out in a long innings, or a short one. In the heyday of our amateur batsmanship we had only to watch Maclaren or R. E. Foster, or Norman Druce, or 'Plum' Warner or R. H. Spooner or

Lionel Ford, to realise at once that here was cricket that gave us a flowering of all the amenities of life enjoyed in the gracious nurseries of cricket—playing-fields far away from the cities and the getting and the spending; House and School games with the chimes of the chapel bell counting the passing hours. There have been 'stylish' professionals, of course: Tom Hayward could have batted in spats and a tall hat. All honour to the poor lad who learns the game in back streets and has to make his living at it almost before he is out of his teens, and yet manages sooner or later to give delight to thousands, as Woolley and Johnny Tyldesley, and 'Patsy' Hendren have done. But the average 'pro.' usually hints of the struggle for existence in mean grasping places. Hammond is majestic, no doubt; but not in the *inherited* way that Maclaren was majestic.

The England XI in the first Test match against the Australians at Birmingham, in 1902, contained Maclaren, Jackson, Ranjitsinhji, Fay and Jessop. Of the professionals in the side, only Tyldesley (the famous 'J.T.' of Lancashire) was picked for his batting alone. Crowds that flocked to Lord's for the match between the Gentlemen and Players looked as a matter of course to the Gentlemen for the really blue-blooded batsmanship. In 1903 the Gentlemen followed on, hopelessly in arrears, against an attack composed of Arnold, Braund, Trott, Hargreave, and John Gunn. They were 244 to the bad when Warner was out, first wicket down. Ranji and Fry then scored 142 in an hour and a half; and after lunch Fry and Maclaren made 309 together in less than three hours, and the innings was then declared closed. The score sheet of this, match shines to-day with a lustre of pomp and affluence:

C B. Fry, not out	232
P. F. Warner, c. Hunter, b. Hargreave	27
K. S. Ranjitsinhji, c. Hunter, b. Gunn.	60
A. C. Maclaren, not out	168
Extras	13
Total (for 2 wkts.)	500

Never since has such batsmanship been seen as this for opulence and prerogative; it was symbolical of the age's prestige. It occurred a year after the Coronation of Edward VII; and it was indeed Coronation cricket, yet one more swaggering pageant reaching to a glittering horizon with Ranji holding the East in fee and bringing to Lord's and London a Kohinoor innings as tribute! Maclaren was the grand manner personified; with his hook-stroke he dismissed the fastest ball from his presence. I have seen him all hauteur though bowled first ball. And Fry, the Sir Willoughby Patterne of the batting crease, handsome and absorbed in himself, not playing the bowling but using it entirely for some private pleasure, a connoisseur in the dialectic of batting. Who will ever forget the cricket ground at Hove in those days, salt tang in the air, and the deck-chairs full, and a stand in progress between Ranji and Fry? East and West twain for hours, the occult and the rational.

There were others amongst the Gentlemen who came into their runs as though by unearned increment, never labourers under the sun. The Hon. F. S. Jackson who batted pure Lombard Street; Beau Nash Palairet, the dashing Stoddart, the prodigy C. L. Townsend—Gilbert Jessop, after Ranji the most inexplicable of the game's phenomena, a scientific hitter, a scorer of runs by hurricane. But there is a calm pivoted place at the centre of the wildest cyclone, and so in an innings by Jessop the fury consumed the field and cried havoc and threatened broken shins and heads and the roofs of houses; but the eye of Jessop and the mind were calm and calculating, the one conveying as swiftly as fine thought the findings of observation to the sure hand that controlled the heavy gunnery. He did not heave his bat from a position far from the ball; in other words he never 'slogged.' He leaped at the overpitched ball rapid and effortless as a panther; he cut the short stuff off the middle stump with his eye and his nose almost dead on the stroke. At the Oval in 1902, England needed 263 to defeat Australia. On a 'turning' pitch five wickets fell for 48, the cream—Maclaren, Palairet, Hayward, Tyldesley, Braund. Then Jackson defended while Jessop actually scored 104 out of 139 in 75 minutes, reducing to a disorganised rabble an Australian XI which until he came in had been monstrous in its calm steely efficiency. Jessop's secret was his ability both to cut and to drive; against these strokes a bowler dare not overtoss or pitch short. But, once again, the technical explanation will not serve. A man achieves by imagination; Jessop, with all his eye and his agile feet and his strokes, could not have won a Test match against odds in an hour if his mind had not envisaged the deed and laughed in advance at impossibilities and hazard. Some of his achievements make fantastical reading nowadays; but they really did happen. Four times he scored a century in both innings of a county match, each time at the rate of 100 an hour. For Gloucestershire against Sussex at Brighton in 1903 he scored 286 in less than three hours; for the Gentlemen of the South and the Players of the South, in 1907 at Hastings, he scored 191 in 90 minutes. It was in 1907 that he demolished the famous 'googly' bowlers from South Africa, the best of all exponents of this kind of spin, and scored 93 from 63 balls. The South African team that year included not only the 'googly' spinners but J. J. Kotze, one of the fastest bowlers of the day. Jessop compelled Kotze to use four outfields. He was conceived and created in the mighty convulsion of energy of genius which, between 1890 and 1914, hurled up all the peaks, the mighty ranges on which repose in unapproachable grandeur the masters of the Golden Age of Cricket.

There were bowlers too. There can be no great batting without great bowling. In the nineties there was a revival of speed, and it attained leonine power and nobility in Tom Richardson. In Lockwood, the destructive force was volcanic—with the volcano's habit of a period of smouldering quiescence followed by a hell-fire consuming eruption. Richardson, a tawny giant, ran to the wicket in long swinging strides, gathering momentum, his leap as the breaking of a wave. Lockwood was more feline and subtler. Richardson's breakback was an honest axe. Lockwood concealed the edge—his slower ball puzzled even Ranji to the end; 'No matter how long I had batted or how many I had made, I could never trust Lockwood; at any moment he would let go the unplayable ball, perhaps not for hours, but you could never be sure.' And while I praise these two Surrey bowlers I must praise with equal reverence and admiration George Lohmann, who was at his greatest for Surrey in the eighties, and died young, just before Richardson's and Lockwood's coming to mastery. W. G. Grace and C. B. Fry were unanimous that Lohmann was the most beautiful and most skilful of all medium-paced bowlers. Nobody has equalled his

J. J. KOTZE
'One of the fastest bowlers of the day.'

average, in Test matches, of 13.01 for 77 wickets. And he was a gallant batsman and a lissome slip-field as quick and certain as any ever known, and a man who was loved at first sight of his fair hair and complexion, and his happy blue eyes.

Nearly every county could boast a fast bowler now; Richardson or Lockwood stood apart, but also there were Mold and W. M. Bradley and S. M. J. Woods; and as the nineteen-hundreds dawned these were followed by W. Brearley, 'Sailor' Young, Wass, Kortright, Fielder, Warren, Bestwick, Frank Field, Woodcock, George Wilson of Worcestershire, all genuinely fast, not merely quick. But this was the zenith of slow and medium bowling, too; there have never been the equals since, for perfection and subtlety of spin and flight, of Blythe, Rhodes, C. L. Townsend, Mead of Essex, Dennett, Barnes, Haigh, F. S. Jackson, J. T. Hearne, Braund, Hallam. And before the new century was in its teens the game was enriched by the greatest of all exponents of the new-fangled 'googly'—Vogler and Faulkner and Pegler and D. W. Carr, not to mention B. J. T. Bosanquet, the first thorough experimenter at the off-break bowled with the action of a leg-break. There was, as well, the greatest of swerve bowlers— George Hirst.

We can say of any of the arts and pastimes of man that it is in its Golden Age when every technical part and potentiality of it are being explored and exhibited, with a masterly exponent for every known department of skill and for every conceivable manifestation of style. Every attribute of the game was consummated by the masters of the 1900's; there was even a superb bowler of lobs. The Golden Age saw cricket *sub specie aeternitatis*; variety of genius revealed all its glories, whether of craftsmanship or characteristic art. It is not possible even in our dreams to conceive of players greater than these that I name herewith, each without a peer in his H. Martyn (perhaps the greatest of English wicket-keepers), Tyldesley, J. T. Brown, R. E. and H. K. Foster, K. L. Hutchings, P. F. Warner, Barnes, Spooner, Palairet, Abel, Rhodes, Blythe, Lockwood, Richardson, George Gunn, Mead of Essex, Arnold, J. W. H. T. Douglas, D. W. Carr, Bosanquet and Simpson-Hayward. Here is cricket in excelsis, from A to Z. And not only have I confined my inventory to Englishmen; I have made it later than Bobby Peel's heyday.

The same full flowering of every actual or conjecturable seed happened in the same period in Australian cricket. We need but mention names: Trumper, Duff, Darling, Clem Hill, Noble, Macartney, S. E. Gregory, Armstrong, Trumble, Ernest Jones, Cotter, Kelly, Carter, Ransford, Bardsley, Hordern. All of them, every cricketer I have mentioned in these lists (and I have been obliged to omit several notable ones) could have been seen in action, often during the same match, on any day of any summer between 1900-1914. There have been great and glorious cricketers since then in this or that direction, style or department, but never has there been the same synthesis of the game's manifold genius, *in every shape and form.*

Talent begets talent; genius is unique and springs from nowhere. The logic of growth and development produces a Hobbs, a Hammond, a Bradman; we can see in their methods the chain of progress; they are reapers of harvests. 'Ranji' was absolutely unique, and after him there was Jessop. Only one other batsman may be said to have shared the absolutely inimitable secret—Victor Trumper (but another Australian, C. G. Macartney, must have touched his mantle). Trumper's cricket burns in my memory to this day with all the glowing forging heat and brilliance of the actual experience of it, the instantaneous ignition. This was the batsmanship of aggression dressed in shining armour. It is remarkable that he did not blind us to the quality of his contemporaries amongst Australians. It is impossible here to praise them all; enough to say that in the Golden Age of English cricket, the Australians were our equals, both as antagonists and as adornments to the art of cricket.

NEXT TO THE REVOLUTION PUT INTO FORCE BY THE first overarm bowling, the most seminal and far-reaching influence in the game's technique was the 'googly,' an off-break bowled with a leg-break turn at the wrist. Bosanquet of Middlesex, the pioneer, was carefully studied by R. O. Schwarz, who also played for Middlesex for a while. He then returned to South Africa and taught the new trick there, and in 1907, the South African bowlers spread perplexity and ruin amongst English players, though they could not win the rubber. Vogler actually contrived the new spin with something of pace. More than anybody else Hobbs mastered this 'new weapon', not only on English turf but on South African matting, where the break did its work quicker and at a nastier angle. The lesson of Hobbs was lost on most of his English colleagues. He mainly countered the 'googly' by forward play, or a quick-footed move to the pitch of it. The others drew back and covered the wickets with their pads, and allowed the left shoulder to swing round to the on, a position from which no strong forward hit can be made. So was born the bane of modern cricket, the so-called 'two-eyed' stance. It was aggravated by the increase in swerve bowling. Years earlier than this, bowlers had caused the ball to swerve through the air, none more so than Hirst of Yorkshire and J. B. King, a Philadelphian. But not until cricket was resumed after

the four years' silence of the first World War did batsmen in bulk slavishly and irrationally place themselves
legs in front of the wicket even for half-volleys, and
often content themselves, until the bowling was dog-
tired, with pushes and pokes to the onside. Certain
players combined clever and often brilliant forcing
strokes with the 'two-eyed stance,' but the ancient
glory began to grow dim; the sun went down on the
Golden Age, and for a long time we were only reminded
of it when an oldish player such as Woolley or Bowley
of Sussex or George Gunn of Nottinghamshire batted
an innings which seemed to catch the last rays of the
afterglow. Quaife of Warwickshire, a notorious though
stylish stonewaller survival from the Golden Age, lived
to discover himself in the 1920's to be as quick a scorer
as most of the exponents of the 'post-war school.' At
his most passive, Quaife in his proper period had made
his centuries at an average rate of four hours each—
'Ranji' and Trumper and Tyldesley and Maclaren and
Spooner and Hutchings and J. N. Crawford seldom if
ever spent as much time in one innings over as niggardly
an amount of runs as that. A century scored during the
1920's in three or four hours was invariably described
by the current newspapers as 'brilliant.' But there was
another and more psychological cause of the general
eclipse. And so, in due or overdue time, our studies
have reached authentic modern cricket—our last lap.

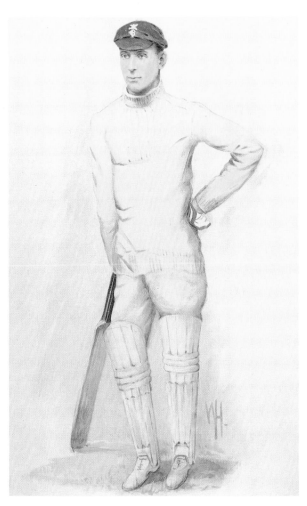

J. B. Hobbs 1912
"A complete synthesis of known principles of batsmanship."

D. G. Bradman 1938
"Grand and exhilarating to watch."

WHEN FIRST-CLASS CRICKET WAS PLAYED AGAIN after the end of the 1914-1918 war, we were given yet another example of what a sensitive plant this cricket is—how quick to respond to atmosphere, how eloquent at any time of the English mood and temper. It was an age of some disillusionment and cynicism; the romantic gesture was distrusted. 'Safety First' was the persistent warning. We saw at once on the cricket field the effect of a dismal philosophy and a debilitated state of national health. Beautiful and brave stroke-play gave way to a sort of trench warfare, conducted behind the sandbag of broad pads. Bowlers came under the same bleak influence; fast bowling on the one hand and slow spin on the other were generally regarded as much too uneconomical. The fast bowler's life was short and arduous and none but the really great could succeed with slow spin on modern turf. A shrewd professionalism decided on a compromise; enough of pace, pitched just short of a length, and a suggestion of spin and more of swerve, the attack directed on the leg-stump—the main idea being to obtain a reasonably good bowling analysis every season at the expenditure of a minimum of risk and physical endurance. The root cause was the nation's economy. There were now few of the amateur players from the old social mint; the example of style and the independent gesture was no longer present

WALTER HAMMOND
'Majestic.'

everywhere and every day. County captains lost the ancient prerogative; like the Duke of Plaza-Toro, they led their regiments from behind—they found it less exciting. If Bloggs of Blankshire wished to complete his 2,000 runs before the end of June he must be allowed to go his patient way to glory; if a record was within reach of breaking-point no cricket captain of the 1920's dare tell his crack 'pro.' to get his runs quickly to-day or get out. The more popular newspapers aggravated the trouble; they extolled huge individual aggregates of runs for the sake of them, with little insistence on individuality of technique or on the honours due to vital, beautiful and hazardous sport.

The discontents grew summer by summer. Armstrong's conquering Australians won eight Test matches consecutively; Australian cricket had remained more or less in touch with the pre-war traditions. In 1921 their batsmen scored prolifically in England at the rate of 90 an hour. An attempt was made by legislators to put an end to negative batting and negative bowling. The height of the stumps was increased; a smaller ball was given to the bowler. Groundsmen were severely lectured in leading articles in *The Times* for thinking there was nothing like rollers. Even the Eton and Harrow match was petrified year by year from the prevalent paralysis; it was seldom finished, or the runs were scored as slowly and by much the same methods as in Lancashire and Yorkshire matches of the period (but Lancashire and Yorkshire matches were once almost rhetorically gallant and romantic!). The source of the disease could not be touched by new laws—these were the remedies of superficially-minded physicians. English cricket in the 1920's was, like the country as a whole, psychologically, even spiritually, ill; character and skill in cricket were becoming standardised, with everything else in the land.

When Maurice Tate bowled in Australia in the Test matches of 1924-1925, it was like the return of the age of giants; he and Larwood are the only two English bowlers produced between the two wars who survive comparison with the best pre-1914 stock.

During 1919-1939, English cricket produced only two players who could have obtained places in an England XI of the early 1900's, for batsmanship alone; they are Hammond and Duleepsinhji. I am aware that statistics can be produced to argue a more flattering case for contemporary achievement; I am aware that statistics maintain that Sutcliffe with an average of 66.85 for 2,741 in Test matches against Australia was a greater player than Tom Hayward who had to be content with an average of 35.65 and 1,747 runs. In style and technical organisation there was no comparison at all between these two cricketers and nobody who remembers both will insist that there was, unless afflicted by sentimentality about the present—and it is a mistake to imagine that it is only thoughts of the past that lead folk to sloppiness. Since 1919 there was undoubtedly an advance in average skill in batting, a consequence not only of a decline in imaginative bowling, but of the fact that there was now more accumulated technique for the ordinarily capable player to learn. The game has lost character; the few really great ones remaining— Bradman, Hammond, Headley, Larwood, O'Reilly, Grimmett, McCabe, Tate—would hold their own in any company of the immortals; the rank-and-file are like poor relations who have surprisingly come into money— by the accident of being born when they were born they have inherited the technical legacy of the Golden Age.

Hobbs, like Grace, arched two periods; he could be related to the Golden Age in the brilliance of his stroke-play from 1905-1914; he was the first to demonstrate the way to play the swerves and the 'googlies.' In all conditions, on English and Australian turf, on the matting of South Africa, he made a complete synthesis of known principles of batsmanship. He was encyclopaedic. There was another player contemporary with him who, against the world's greatest bowler and on the difficult matting of his own country exhibited a technique as masterful and as modern as Bradman's: I refer to H. W. Taylor.

The advent of Bradman was inevitable—the logical consequence of Hobbs' accumulation of skill; or if I may use so strong a term in a book about cricket— the Hobbs synthesis. His record in England *v.* Australia matches is prodigious: 3,840 runs, average 91.42. He has combined defensive play off the back foot with attack that seldom loses sight of the ball; rarely do you see him compelled to lunge forward speculatively; the secret of his mastery is that by swift judgement and swift feet he can always make the length he needs for the execution of his wide range of strokes. Added to technique which summarises all experience from 'Ranji' onwards, is the 'new' and mechanistic theory that every ball is the first ball and that when you have completed one hundred runs you begin again. Efficiency, superb stream-lined efficiency! And, don't mistake me, Bradman is often grand and exhilarating to watch. But if I were asked to compare him with Trumper I should say the difference is as that between the flight of the aeroplane and the flight of an eagle.

It is certain, and can be deduced almost mathematically or geometrically, that Bradman's records will be surpassed before we are much older unless a new problem is put by the bowlers, or unless rude nature in the turf is allowed again to assert herself. In 1938 young Hutton of Yorkshire beat Bradman's total of 334 in a Test match. The *reductio ad absurdum* of contemporary mechanical run-making occurred in South Africa. South Africa went in first and scored 530, and England responded with 316. In the second innings South Africa reached 481 which left England with 696 to win. They made 654 of them, for five wickets only, but there wasn't time to finish the curious proceedings; the English team had to catch a boat back home. The match lasted nine days, and the rate of scoring was imperceptible; sometimes it averaged less than 20 an hour on a flawless wicket. Anybody with eyes not blind, using a straight bat, could pick up a century, if only he denied the spirit of sport.

The rumpus about the Larwood form of attack (so-called 'bodyline') was a desperate remedy in the face of the robot batsman. But it was directed mainly against Bradman, by no means a robot, and never reluctant to answer the challenge of anybody's attack. Larwood, one of the fastest and most accurate bowlers ever known, exploited a field set mainly on the leg-side, in a semi-circle near the batsman's left hip, with two men placed deep. The ball was delivered at a terrific velocity, pitched short enough to rise, three or four times an over, in the region of the batsman's skull. If he merely shielded himself, and 'found contact,' the crouching inner field caught the ball as it fell from his protective bat. If he desperately 'hooked' or 'pulled,' he was most times caught from a great stroke on the leg-boundary. By grace of fortune and a brave heart and good vision, McCabe actually scored 187 not out at Sydney in 1932 against Larwood and the leg-trap.

This species of bowling temporarily reduced Bradman's batting average to the 50's, and won a rubber. But fast body-line, good enough for Bradman in the land of the barbarian, was quickly frowned upon when the conquering Larwood returned home and others sought to emulate his methods on the playing fields of England. None the less Larwood for a season solved the problem of years—how to put an end to the mechanical domination of the batsman on a perfect pitch. Was it not cricket? Is there not an order of ethics higher than the common one? No doubt a whole race of Larwoods would have put an end to cricket altogether as an art and a controlled science. But, judged by the measure of genius applied by the amoral gods, Larwood's attack in Australia was wonderful, thrilling and beautiful to behold.

Another world war interrupted the stalemate. When the game 'begins again' let us hope it will renew itself, like Antaeus, by contact with the ancient earth— in other words, by going back to natural English turf. There is, after all, always the example before us of club cricket; the decadent perfection of the 'modern' Test match has not affected bold enterprise and heroism on the village cricket fields of the Little Puddletons, where the wicket may easily be planted, as at old Hambledon, on the brow of a hill, where the ball behaves according to no predictable science of curves, angles, flights and gyrations, and batsmen feel 'set' when they have broken their ducks and begin to hit after they have surprisingly attained double figures.

And not only should the groundsman be ordered to make a fair wicket with as little preparation as is consistent with conditions of local soil rolled to reliability but not to lifelessness; also the factor of time must be retained in great matches. The players must be up and doing, conscious that they are under a lease of hours, and that they must not let their wits sleep or wander, they must always be aware that the clock in the pavilion may be an ally or an enemy, unless constantly propitiated. But most of all it is the spirit that counts. Cricket, as we saw in the first pages of our book, is a game dependent more than any other on the character and idealism of the players. The Golden Age will not be brought back by legislation, by any arbitrary change in the rules and the material conditions of the game. Whatever the circumstances, heavy roller or no heavy roller, perfect wicket or imperfect, the ignoble stalemate at Durban in 1939, and other travesties of sport of the same order, could not have happened with players of the breed of Maclaren, Trumper, Macartney, Constantine, and George Hirst. Even without a time limit, it was possible once for England and Australia—on perfect Australian wickets— to fight the good fight chivalrously and decisively. In the long run the game is the sum total of the character of the men who take part in it. Negation on the field of play indicates negation of mind and soul. The style and the spirit are the cricketers themselves.

Short Bibliography

Great Batsmen and Great Bowlers and Fielders by G. W. Beldam and C. B. Fry; *Cricket Country* by Edmund Blunden; *Cricket and Australian Summer* by Neville Cardus; *Lord's and the M.C.C.* by G. R. C. H. Harris and F. S. Ashley-Cooper; *Jubilee Book* by K. S. Ranjitsinhji; *My Cricketing Life*; *Cricket Between Two Wars* and *The Book of Cricket*, 1945 edition, by Sir Pelham F. Warner; *Memorial Biography of Grace*, 1848-1915

colour plates

Lords and Gentlemen of Surrey and Kent playing at
Knole Park, Kent, 1775

Cricket match between Nottingham and Leicester,
c. 1829

W. G. Grace

F. R. Spofforth

G. L. Jessop

K. S. Ranjitsinhji

J. B. Hobbs

D. G. Bradman

black & white illustrations

The Noble Game of Cricket – an illustration from 1857

Joseph Guy, 1857

Four Surrey Cricketers, 1852

Alfred Mynn, 1852

Lord's Cricket Ground, 1837

The Victorian Game – a match between Kent and Sussex at Brighton

The Draw – from a series of batting cartoons, 1845

An XI of England V. XXII of Victoria at Melbourne, 1864

The Australians V. Thorton's XI at Orleans House

Victor Trumper

Run Out – an illustration by Ernest Prater, 1902

J. J. Kotze

Walter Hammond

Index

Birmingham 31, 70

Bradman, D. G. 7, 15, 17, 37, 78, 85-88

Bristol 36, 43-44

Brown of Brighton 19, 29

Clarke, Charles Cowden 14

Clarke, William 16, 19

Daft, Richard 24, 26, 33, 40

Denton, David 20

Dickens, Charles 39

Dumkins, Mr 20

Emmett, Tom 33

Gentlemen of Sussex 36

Gloucestershire 10, 41

Grace, W. G. 10, 33, 36-56, 60, 76

Gunn, William 65

Guy, Joseph 16

Hambeldon 12-14, 18, 20-21, 23, 89

Hammond 9, 15, 37, 70, 78, 84-85

Harris, David 14, 19-20

Hobbs 32, 65, 77-79, 85-86

Hornby, A. N. 10

Humphreys, Walter 20

Jackson, John 21, 35

Jephson, A. 20

Jessop, Gilbert 72-74, 77-78

Kennington 8

Kent 13-14, 18, 23-24

Kotze, J. J. 74

Lancashire 7, 23, 52

94

Larwood 15, 23
Leeds 8, 31
Lillywhite 18, 34 35, 77
Lockyer, Tom 10
Lord, Thomas 29
Lord's 8, 9, 24, 27-29, 31-32, 51-52, 60, 64, 70-71
Ludd, Master 21
Luffey, Mr 20
Maclaren, A. C. 20
Middlesex 31, 41, 60, 79
Mozart, Wolfgang 16
Mynn, Alfred 19, 24, 26
Norfolk 23, 31
Nottingham 34, 51
Nyren, John 14
Nyren, Richard 14
Oval 32, 45, 53, 56
Parr, George 35
Platt 24
Prowse, W. J. 26

Ranjitsinhji, K. S. 37, 43, 64, 69, 70, 72, 74, 77, 78, 80, 86
Reigate 12
Rhodes, Wilfred 8
Robinson, Emmott 8, 16
Shaw, Alfred 33, 39
Shrewsbury, Arthur 63
Sinclair, J. H. 20
Small, John 13
Wisden, John 21
Yorkshire 7, 8, 23

Acknowledgments

PRION HAVE ENDEAVOURED TO OBSERVE THE LEGAL requirements with regard to the rights of suppliers of illustrative material and would like to thank Mary Evans Picture Library and Hulton Getty for their generous assistance.